Aluminium

Sally Morgan and Pauline Lalor

WHY WASTE IT?

SIMON & SCHUSTER
YOUNG BOOKS

WHY WASTE IT? has been researched and compiled by Simon & Schuster Young Books. We are very grateful for the support and guidance provided by our advisory panel of professional educationalists in the course of the production.

Advisory panel:
Colin Pidgeon, Headteacher
Wheatfields Junior School, St Albans
Deirdre Walker, Deputy headteacher
Wheatfields Junior School, St Albans
Judith Clarke, Headteacher
Grove Infants School, Harpenden

A catalogue record for this book
is available from the British Library
ISBN 0 7500 1091 6

Commissioning editor: Daphne Butler
Book editor: Claire Llewellyn
Design: M&M Design Partnership
Photographs: Ecoscene except for page 8 Zefa.
Line artwork: Raymond Turvey

First published in Great Britain in 1992
by Simon & Schuster Young Books

Reprinted in 1994

Simon & Schuster Young Books
Campus 400, Maylands Avenue
Hemel Hempstead, Herts HP2 7EZ

Printed and bound in Singapore
by Kim Hup Lee Printing Co.

Contents

Aluminium is a metal

Metals are materials which are often hard and shiny, and can bend. Iron, steel and aluminium are all metals.

Aluminium is a grey metal which is very light in weight.

Can you see anything in the picture which could be made from aluminium?

AEG
7up
Total

Aluminium from bauxite

Aluminium is not a metal which is found in the earth. It is made from a special rock, called bauxite.

People dig up bauxite from mines. At a factory, machines crush the rock and then heat it. This changes the bauxite into aluminium.

Do you know of any other materials which are found in mines?

Aluminium has many uses

If you look around your home, you may find several things which are made from aluminium. It is a very useful material because it is light, and can be bent into different shapes.

What things in the picture are made from aluminium? Why do you think aluminium was chosen in each case?

diet
Coca-Cola

Drinks in aluminium cans

Cans make good containers for drinks. Germs can't get inside, so the drink stays clean and fresh. Fizzy drinks keep their fizz.

Aluminium cans are light to carry. They won't weigh you down on a walk.

Do you think canned drinks are easy to transport from factories to shops? Why?

Aluminium or steel?

Not all cans are made from aluminium. Some are made from a different metal, called steel. Steel is magnetic. How can you prove this?

What happens when you put a magnet near an aluminium can?

Which of the cans in the pictures are made from aluminium?

330 ml
H33/6

CONTAINS ONLY NATURAL FLAVOURS
330 ml
It can only aid slimming or weight control as part of an energy (calorie) controlled diet
100% Aspartame, No Saccharin
INGREDIENTS: CARBONATED WATER, CITRIC ACID, FLAVOURING, ACIDITY REGULATOR: SODIUM CITRATE; ARTIFICIAL SWEETENER: ASPARTAME; PRESERVATIVE: SODIUM BENZOATE; STABILISER: CMC
PRODUCED FOR J SAINSBURY plc
STAMFORD STREET LONDON SE1 9LL

SAFEGUARD
ENVIRONMENT –
FUTURE GENERATIONS
CANS
CANS
CO. LTD
SKIP

Aluminium can be recycled

Some people throw away their old aluminium cans. Do you? Old cans can't be refilled, but the aluminium in them can be used to make new cans. This is called recycling.

Many towns have can banks – big bins just for cans. Are there any in your town?

Recycling aluminium cans

First, the cans are sorted to make sure they are made of aluminium, and not steel. Can you think of a way of doing this?

Next, the cans are put into a machine which squashes them into bales
This makes them easier to transport.

Lastly, the bales are weighed to see how much aluminium is in them.

Sunkist
Vimto
COLA
diet Coke
BITTER
diet Sprite

The squashed cans are melted

Have you ever watched butter melt in a hot saucepan? Metal will melt, too, but only when it is very, very hot.

The bales of squashed cans are heated at a factory until they melt. Then, as the melted aluminium cools and begins to go hard again, it is made into large, thin sheets of metal.

What can be made from the sheets of aluminium?

Recycling helps the rainforest

Bauxite is usually found in hot, tropical places. This is where rainforests grow.

When bauxite is mined, rainforests are cut down. If we keep on mining bauxite, we will destroy more and more of the forest.

Do you know why rainforests are important? How can recycling cans help them?

Recycling saves electricity

You cannot see electricity but you can see what it does. How many ways do you use electricity in your home?

When aluminium is made from bauxite, huge amounts of electricity are used. Recycling uses much less.

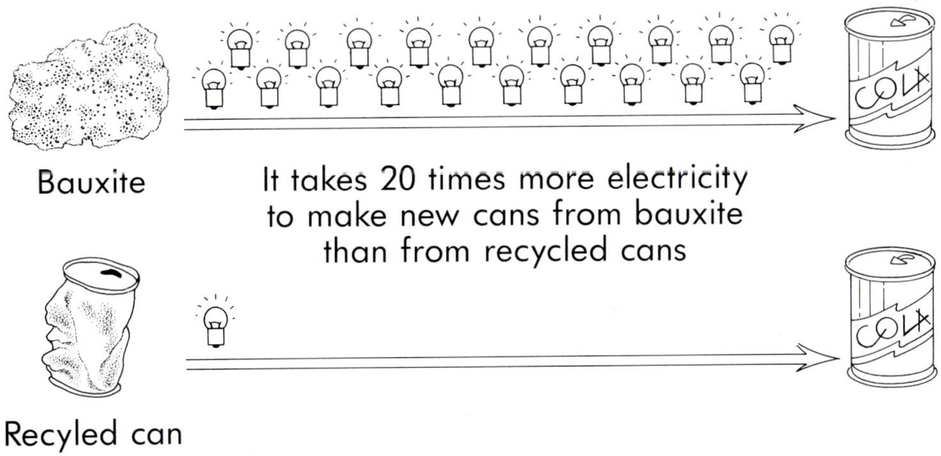

It takes 20 times more electricity to make new cans from bauxite than from recycled cans

Don't drop it – recycle it!

Too many aluminium cans become litter on the streets and in the countryside.

Litter is dirty and unattractive.
Even worse, empty cans are dangerous for small animals which crawl inside, and then get trapped.

Coke
Coke

Money from old cans

Did you know that old aluminium cans are worth money? Many countries pay people for every can they return to the collection points.

Why not collect cans at your school? Where would be the best place for the can bank? What could you buy with the money you raise?

alu
ALUMINIUM
DRINKS CAN
RECYCLING POINT
REDUCE WASTE RAISE MONEY
LOOK FOR THE SYMBOL OR TEST SIDE WITH MAGNET
ALUMINIUM CANS ONLY PLEASE

Index